WHY I CREATED THIS PROG...

During the last several years, I ha...   I have
earned to give thanks for everythi...   I have
earned that having gratitude char...   _reased
my compassion for others.

This program was born out of the love and gratitude that I have experienced from a very special event-- one that has become my annual ritual. For the last several years, I have returned to my undergraduate alma mater, Northwestern University, for homecoming. I love the people I met during college, more than 30 years ago, and they have become dear friends. What is so special for me is that my friends have known me since I was 18 years old and they totally accept me and I accept them. We have supported one another at low points in our lives and we have celebrated the high points together. I feel safe being vulnerable and completely open with this group. I am so grateful to have these special relationships in my life. Over the course of the homecoming weekend, whether it is over a before heading to campus, a quiet conversation at a tailgate, or walking to a happy hour gathering, there is always time to connect with a friend about what is happening in our lives. There is active listening and sound advice exchanged with one another. I am grateful for these bonds that have been forged and strengthened over the years. It is a unique and special experience.

When I go back to homecoming, I am filled with the love, support, hugs, laughter and tears that come from reconnecting with this small group that continue to return every year. I always look forward to being together and participating in the rituals we have created. I've found that by the end of each homecoming weekend, we have what I call a 'love hangover'. We all agree that our love hangover stems from the deep connections that we have created and continue to hold on to every year at homecoming.

My experience in October 2016 was a turning point for me. I felt so grateful to have these people and experiences in my life and so lucky to be able to afford to travel back to my school each homecoming weekend. I understood and realized that there were times in practice when I didn't have the resources to go. I felt grateful to have these wonderful people as friends and to have them support me in everything I was trying to accomplish. I was so full of love that I wanted to take this experience and put it into a vehicle to share my gratitude with others.

From that idea, this gratitude program was born. I dedicated the month of November to a 30 days of this program. Each day, I sent one email out and asked people to join in the experience of *Change your Health and Attitude through Gratitude: A 30 Dae by Dae Guide*. I share this program with you now as it has been updated, revised and become more beautiful over time. My hope for you is that you enjoy it as much as those who have taken journey before you.

In the last 18 years the focus of my work has been supporting women in their journeys to health and healing. Even though these activities may seem to focus more on women, they can be used by anyone.

I believe that everyone, especially women, can create more joyful, purposeful lives when they put their health first. When health becomes your number one priority, you are better able to show up more powerfully in your life and in the lives of those you love.

With that, I am grateful for you and your commitment to making yourself a priority for a few minutes each day over the next month.

To Your One Sweet Life,
Dr. Dae

— DAY 1 —

"Thank you" is a powerful way to share your gratitude with others.

Saying thank you is one of the simplest ways to share gratitude.

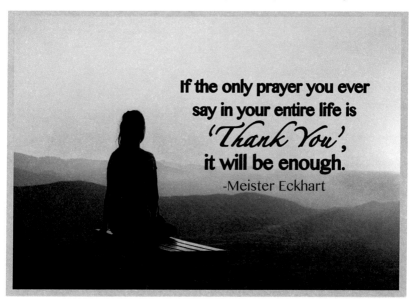

If the only prayer you ever say in your entire life is 'Thank You', it will be enough.
-Meister Eckhart

Today I am grateful for...

DAY 1 : GRATITUDE ACTIVITY

Say Thank You

Everyone loves to feel appreciated and loved! You do, don't you? Well, share that feeling with someone else. Take a few minutes out of your day today to thank someone AND tell them why!

If you have the chance, tell them face-to-face. If not, call them on the phone. Connect with them personally so you can see the smile on their face and the lift in their step after you have shared your gratitude with them. It is amazing how a few kind words, like "thank you", can change not only their outlook but your own as well.

Don't get intimidated by the idea that you have to make some big gesture. It can be as simple as walking up to a friend and saying, "Susan I really appreciate that you pick up the mail when we are out of town. It feels good to know that is taken care of when we are away. Thank you".

So simple!

— DAY 2 —

Gratitude opens the heart to create more space for love to enter into it.

Writing in a journal is a way to express your gratitude and create memories at the same time.

Gratitude is the memory of the heart.
-Jean Baptiste Massieu

Today I am grateful for...

DAY 2 : GRATITUDE ACTIVITY

A Gratitude Journal

Create a special journal to keep track of what you are grateful for. Each morning, before you start your day, write down five things that you are grateful for in your life. It can be a simple list of a few words or phrases to express your thoughts.

Here is a sample for you:
- Breathing
- My family who love and support me
- My friends who make me laugh
- An invitation from my niece to her violin recital
- The lovely dinner my friend cooked for me last night

Alternatively, if you have trouble sleeping at night, write your list before you go to bed instead of first thing in the morning. Take a few deep breaths, relax and focus on what is good in your life. Then write down your five things before you go to bed. See if in 30 days your sleep hasn't improved!

— DAY 3 —

Take a walk in nature today

Nature has an incredible power to calm and relax our
body and mind.

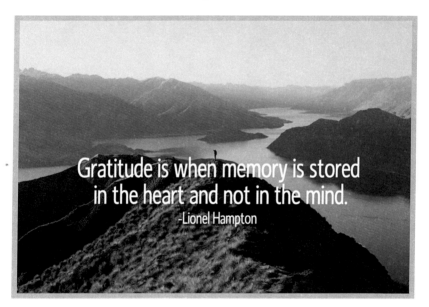

Gratitude is when memory is stored
in the heart and not in the mind.
-Lionel Hampton

Today I am grateful for...

DAY 3 : GRATITUDE ACTIVITY

Take a moment to be grateful for beauty in nature

Every year my family goes to the beach for a week. It is one of my favorite events of the year. When my niece was small, maybe three or four years old, I would walk her to the beach. We would stop at every flower, look at it and smell it. It was so much fun for us to take 20 minutes to walk one block and just enjoy nature. I want you to experience that same joy today.

Take a walk in nature today, 15 or 20 minutes if possible! Use your walk to feel grateful that your arms and legs function so that you can walk. Be grateful to your heart and lungs for allowing you to breath in fresh air. Be grateful for your eyes that you can see all the beauty of the outdoors.

If the weather is bad, find a window and look out of it for five minutes. Look to see trees, leaves, birds, rain or snow in a new way.

— DAY 4 —

Love and appreciate yourself

When we are able to appreciate anything about ourselves, we will be kinder and more gentle in all of our interactions.

Gratitude is the sweet fragrance of an opening heart.
-Aine Belton

Today I am grateful for...

DAY 4 : GRATITUDE ACTIVITY

Focus on your strengths

One of the most important things we can do is to have gratitude for our unique gifts, talents and skills! We should love and appreciate ourselves.

We must acknowledge that each of us has unique gifts, talents and skills to share with the world. If we forget to use our strengths, we are not serving ourselves, our families or our communities well. Today, I want you to write down a list of at least 20 of your strengths!

Please honor this request and come up with a minimum list of 20. Don't cheat yourself and do less! If you have trouble coming up with 20, enlist your friends or family to help you. Once you have completed your list, put it somewhere where you can easily see it and be reminded of your many strengths.

— DAY 5 —

What are five things you are grateful for?

Having visual reminders during the day is one of the best ways to keep something on top of our minds.

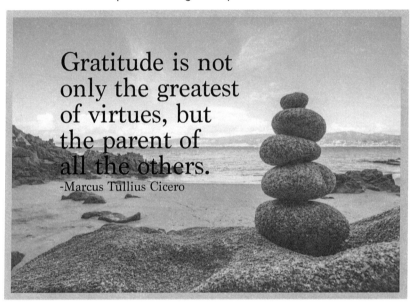

Gratitude is not only the greatest of virtues, but the parent of all the others.
-Marcus Tullius Cicero

Today I am grateful for...

DAY 5 : GRATITUDE ACTIVITY

Post-It Notes

When I was young, post-it notes were introduced for the first time. I loved posting them all over my room just because I liked to be able to stick something to the wall and not get in trouble with my parents for it!

The purpose of post-it notes is to remind you of something. So, they are perfect for reminding you to be grateful and thankful on a daily basis.

For today's activity, I'm going to ask you to get out your post-it notes and write five things that you are grateful for. Post quotes and images around your house that remind you to be grateful. Once you have written the post-it notes, put each one in a place where you will see it every day.

Some good places are:

• on the bathroom mirror or wall
• on the refrigerator
• on the dashboard of your car
• on the screen of your desktop computer at work

Get creative about where you will notice your post-it notes every day to remind you to be grateful. If you really like that idea, then consider using more decorative - paper or cardstock and write your gratitude thoughts on it. Tape or even frame them to make them more permanent.

— DAY 6 —

Be grateful that you have food to eat.

Sometimes we take our most basic activities for granted.

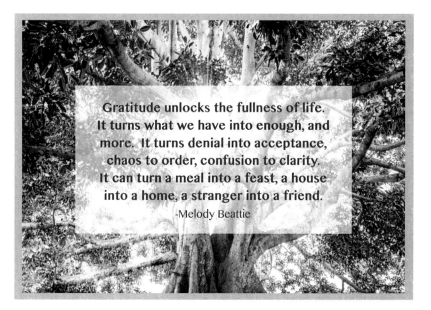

Gratitude unlocks the fullness of life.
It turns what we have into enough, and
more. It turns denial into acceptance,
chaos to order, confusion to clarity.
It can turn a meal into a feast, a house
into a home, a stranger into a friend.
-Melody Beattie

Today I am grateful for...

DAY 6 : GRATITUDE ACTIVITY

Cooking is Love

Once a year, my meditation group gets together to celebrate our friendship and fellowship. We have a potluck where everyone brings a contribution to our meal. We celebrate new adventures and accomplishments that we have achieved as well as tough times that we've navigated through. We are so grateful for each other's presence and for the time we have together.

Over the years, our meditation group has become very close as we sit together in meditation. We nourish or minds and our souls together. During our yearly potluck, we take time to nourish our bodies together. It is a wonderful way to nourish ourselves in a way that is different from our normal connection. Eating together in community can bring people together in ways you might never imagine.

For today's gratitude activity, I am inviting you to cook a meal with love for yourself or someone you know and love. As you cook your meal think about the people you are feeding. If you are part of a family, ask family members to cook with you. If you live alone, consider inviting someone to cook or eat with you. If you know someone who is not feeling well or, who lives alone or, might just need some special care, consider taking a meal to them.

Be grateful that you have food to eat! For some people, eating every day is not a given!

— DAY 7 —

Writing is a powerful way to remind us of what's important.

When you write something down it locks the key idea into your brain.

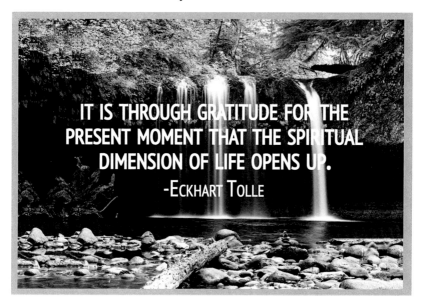

IT IS THROUGH GRATITUDE FOR THE PRESENT MOMENT THAT THE SPIRITUAL DIMENSION OF LIFE OPENS UP.
-ECKHART TOLLE

Today I am grateful for...

DAY 7 : GRATITUDE ACTIVITY

A Bowl Full of Gratitude

Writing something down is a powerful way to remind us of what is important. This is why the gratitude journal works so well. Here is a fun, creative way to look at your gratitude journal. It is one of my favorite activities because it is a gift that keeps on giving.

Today, I'm asking you to write down on slips of paper some of the things you are grateful for and put them into a clear bowl or vase. You can add something that you are grateful for every day. Then, when you are having a bad or difficult day, you can reach into your clear bowl and pull out the beautiful memory of something you are grateful for.

It is a great way to change your mindset from the grimness of a challenging day to the joy of a grateful and thankful one, past or present!

— DAY 8 —

Each of your successes, big or small, are worth celebrating!

The act of celebration releases happy chemicals in the brain called endorphins, which improve not only the mood but also immune and body functions.

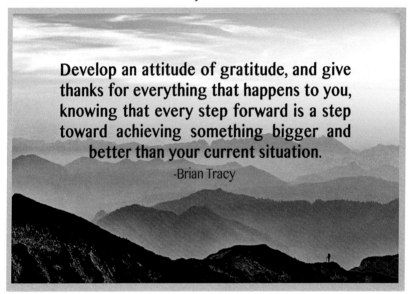

Develop an attitude of gratitude, and give thanks for everything that happens to you, knowing that every step forward is a step toward achieving something bigger and better than your current situation.
-Brian Tracy

Today I am grateful for...

DAY 8 : GRATITUDE ACTIVITY

Reflect on your Success

The beginning of something can seem really hard. But when you take it step by step, you can achieve anything.

There is a sweet success in achieving something that you think is out of your reach. We've all had success like that! Did you take the time to celebrate that success? Today you will!

Today, I want you to reflect on a project that you have accomplished, preferably one in the last three months. This project perhaps was one that was challenging for you at the beginning but you accomplished successfully.

Take a few minutes and feel the joy and thankfulness you have for completing that project! You might feel grateful just for the fact that you have completed it! Or perhaps you are grateful because you didn't think you would get through it but you did!

The most successful people in the world are the people that take stock of their successes on a consistent basis. It is not in a boastful way, but it is a way to develop confidence and focus to continue to move forward.

— DAY 9 —

Give thanks for the things that ARE working in your body.

A powerful mindfulness exercise is to focus on what is going right in our bodies. Our brains tend towards negative thoughts about 70% of the time, so they are designed to counteract our normal brain functions.

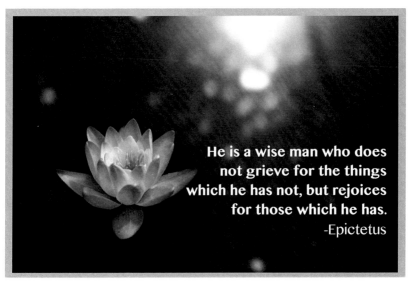

He is a wise man who does not grieve for the things which he has not, but rejoices for those which he has.
-Epictetus

Today I am grateful for...

DAY 9 : GRATITUDE ACTIVITY

Grateful for Your Body

Have you stopped to say thank you to your body for all the ways in which it works correctly and seamlessly? Today is your day to be grateful for the things that ARE working in your body!

As a doctor, it is part of my job to hear about the problems our bodies experience. It is easy to focus on our aches, pains and illnesses but do we ever stop to think about all the things that are working perfectly in our bodies today?

I have a friend that works in a hospital and whenever I go to see him, I notice all the people in the halls that are hooked up to tubes, missing limbs or in wheelchairs and it fills me with such gratitude for my good health.

When we have good health, we tend to take it for granted but it is really such a blessing! I am so grateful that my body continues to function well.

For today's gratitude activity, take this opportunity to say thank you to every part of your body that works and supports your ability to do your daily activities.

Simply take a minute to close your eyes and take deep breaths. Scan each part of your body and softly say "thank you" one body part at a time.

— DAY 10 —

Take a break and get inspired!

It seems counterintuitive to stop working, especially when we are unmotivated or frustrated about our work. But, taking a break can revive our ability to be inspired about our work.

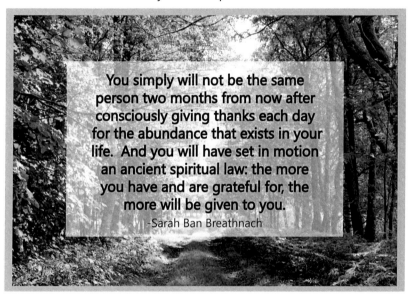

You simply will not be the same person two months from now after consciously giving thanks each day for the abundance that exists in your life. And you will have set in motion an ancient spiritual law: the more you have and are grateful for, the more will be given to you.
-Sarah Ban Breathnach

Today I am grateful for...

DAY 10 : GRATITUDE ACTIVITY

Be Inspired

When it comes to surfing the internet, Ted.com and YouTube.com are some of my favorite places to take a break and get inspired. Watching an inspirational video clip or movie can really help me feel so grateful for my life. It can remind me of the amazing skills and talents that exist out there that I can share with others. It can motivate me to be kinder or gentler with myself and with others.

I am fortunate that in my research I've come across so many wonderful, inspirational stories that help me stay grateful for the many things, both big and small, that I have in my life.

Today, I'm suggesting that you watch an inspirational video. Many are only five minutes or less. Or, if you have a little more time, about 18 minutes, then I recommend a Ted Talk. Some of them are amazing and they cover every topic imaginable.

— DAY 11 —

Whose presence in your life makes you feel happy?

In times when we're feeling down or discouraged, friends and family can be strong source of inspiration to keep us in a positive frame of mind and continue towards our goals.

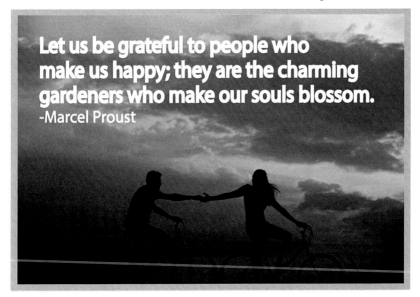

Let us be grateful to people who make us happy; they are the charming gardeners who make our souls blossom.
-Marcel Proust

Today I am grateful for...

DAY 11 : GRATITUDE ACTIVITY

Grateful for a Mentor

When you are happy, have you noticed how much energy you have? How much compassion do you have for others? Or the way you see beauty in every moment? Happiness is something that comes from within but there are definitely people who help bring it out in us.

Today is a great day to think about those people whose presence makes you feel happy.

On the first day, I asked you to say thank you to someone and tell them why. Today I am going to ask you to go a little deeper. I want you to take a few moments to think about a time when you were feeling down or discouraged and someone lifted you up with a kind word or advice that set you on the right track.

Perhaps it was a teacher, friend, mentor, boss or co-worker that noticed that you were having a bad moment and said something that changed your attitude and helped you get back on the right track. Reach out and thank them for their help.

This exercise is a gift not only to yourself but to them as well. They might not even be aware of how they helped you during that time!

— DAY 12 —

Gratitude can improve your immune system and health!

Studies show that gratitude improves the immune system.

Gratitude is a vaccine, an antitoxin and an antiseptic.
-John Henry Jowett

Today I am grateful for...

DAY 12 : GRATITUDE ACTIVITY

Smile!

Gratitude actually changes our health! It impacts not only our mental health but our physical health as well. So, gratitude can even fend off colds and flu! In fact, it can improve so many bodily functions.

Today is a fun day to smile. Have you ever noticed that when you smile at someone it encourages people to smile back at you? I want you to practice smiling all day today!

What makes you smile? Think of something or someone that makes you genuinely happy and your face will automatically break into a smile.

Here are a couple of ways you can increase the number of times you smile during the day:

• Set an alarm on your phone or computer and every time it goes off, think of something that makes you happy. You will smile instantly!
• Every time you go through a doorway or get in or out of the car, smile.
• Smile at every person you walk by today.

— DAY 13 —

Be gratefil for the time and capacity to play!

Children have a huge capacity to live in the present and laugh and play spontaneously.

HAPPINESS
is itself a kind of gratitude.
-JOSEPH WOOD KRUTCH

Today I am grateful for...

DAY 13 : GRATITUDE ACTIVITY

Play Like a Kid Again

Children have an incredible capacity to be happy. They can always see the world in new and creative ways. Let's look through the eyes of a child to remember happiness.

I want you to think about a time in your childhood when you were happy. Think about the activities that you used to do as a child that made you happy. Now, write down 8 activities that used to make you happy when you were a child.

Here is my list:
• Running around in the backyard barefooted
• Playing marbles
• Swapping secrets with my friends
• Smelling the roses
• Baking cookies
• Taking baths
• Picking tomatoes off the vine at Florence's house
• Playing in the sprinkler in the summer

Once you have your list, pick one and make time to do it in the next few days. Basically, I want you to play like you are a child again. Feel the joy and happiness of the fun you had as a child. You can even do it with your own children if you have them. Be grateful for the time and capacity to play!

— DAY 14 —

Sharing needs to come from the heart.

If you are really thankful, what do you do? **You share**.
-*W. Clement Stone*

Today I am grateful for...

DAY 14 : GRATITUDE ACTIVITY

Sharing is Caring

One of the things I love about children is that they love to share. Have you ever been around toddlers and noticed how they share everything they have? If they have a soggy cheerio, they will likely share it with you. It's sweet and a little gross at the same time. The point is that whatever they have they are willing to share, no matter how small or insignificant.

Today I want you to share something you have with someone you know. It doesn't have to be an expensive or elaborate share. It just needs to come from the heart.

Share food - Bring an extra piece of fruit to lunch and give it to a coworker.

Share a pen - Fish one out of your purse if you notice someone struggling to find a pen at a meeting and give it to them.

Share a link to a free online class – As things are opening up, there are so many great classes that are free. Share one with someone that would appreciate it.

Find a way to share something you have with someone who needs something.

— DAY 15 —

Honor others by looking at their photograph and feeling gratitude for them.

When you allow yourself to remember the feelings of gratitude you have for someone, it calms down your nervous system.

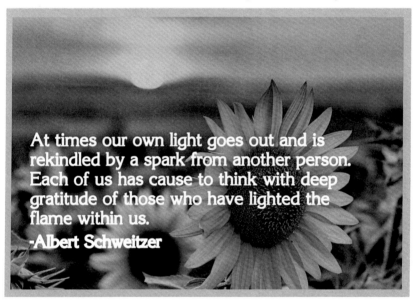

At times our own light goes out and is rekindled by a spark from another person. Each of us has cause to think with deep gratitude of those who have lighted the flame within us.
-Albert Schweitzer

Today I am grateful for...

DAY 15 : GRATITUDE ACTIVITY

Beautiful Photos

As humans, we live in a community. We were not meant to live alone.

In those moments when we feel really alone, having the love and support of other people is invaluable.

Today I want you to look through photos to find one of someone who has lifted you up during a tough time in your life. Perhaps it is a parent, grandparent, sibling, friend, classmate or church member.

Put the photo of this special person in a special place. If it's a digital photo, make it your desktop or screen saver photo. If you are able, print or frame it and display it where you can see it often.

It is a great way to honor those people by looking at them and feeling gratitude for them throughout the day.

P.S. I wanted to let you know that if you don't have time to do one of these gratitude activities, be forgiving and gentle with yourself. These are designed to be helpful ideas to get you thinking about gratitude. Whatever you do, have gratitude in your heart and it will be perfect.

— DAY 16 —

Share gratitude with people you don't know well.

Metta meditation can be used as a practice of sending loving kindness to people that you don't know well.

> When we become more fully aware that our success is due in large measure to the loyalty, helpfulness and encouragement we have received from others, our desire grows to pass on similar gifts. Gratitude spurs us on to prove ourselves worthy of what others have done for us. The spirit of gratitude is a powerful energizer."
> — Wilferd A. Peterson

Today I am grateful for...

DAY 16:

Sharing with Others

Now that you are in the swing of gratitude, I'm going to ask you to share gratitude with people whom you don't know very well.

In my meditation group, we have a practice of sending loving kindness both to people we love and to people we don't know. Today, I'm going to ask you to practice an attitude of gratitude to someone you don't know. Say thank you to them.

Here are a couple of examples of how you can do this:

• If you have to call the computer tech to help you with something on your computer, when the project is finished send him or her an email to say thank you.
• If you are in the grocery store thank the cashier and the person who bags your groceries or carries them to your car. Tell them how much you appreciate their help.
• If someone from the PTA calls about a meeting, say thank you for the reminder.

It's that simple!

— DAY 17 —

How many people do you thank each day?

Being social and increasing your interactions can help you feel kindness.

Find the good and
praise it.
-Alex Haley

Today I am grateful for...

DAY 17: GRATITUDE ACTIVITY

Thank you all day long

Today, we are going to be ambitious!

We are going to expand on our earlier exercise of 'sharing gratitude with a stranger' by saying thank you to not one but **10** people you don't know.

Now, I know you're thinking, "Dr. Dae, 10 people is a lot!", but this is actually more simple than you think. For instance, you can thank someone for holding the door or elevator for you. Thank the waiter for bringing you something you asked for. Thank the bus or uber driver when you get out of the vehicle. Thank the barista for your coffee.

If you are not interacting with many people, you can leave a sign on the door for the mail carrier or delivery person. You can think about groups that you belong to and thank the tech person setting up the meeting or the secretary for sending you notes when you couldn't attend.

Are you starting to get the picture?

At the end of the day, notice if you were more social than usual. Do you have more energy at the end of the day?

— DAY 18 —

Just do something nice.

Endorphins are the chemical messengers for kindness
and relaxation.

Happiness cannot be
traveled to, owned, earned,
worn or consumed.
Happiness is the spiritual
experience of living every
minute with love, grace and
gratitude.
-Denis Waitley

Today I am grateful for...

DAY 18 : GRATITUDE ACTIVITY

An Act of Kindness

Did you know that when you do a kind act for someone it increases endorphins, the happy chemical, in your brain? It also increases endorphins in the brain of the person you helped.

What is amazing is that studies show that people who witness an act of kindness increase their level of endorphins as well!

Today, I would like you to perform a random act of kindness. It can be to another person, animal or even a plant! The definition of kindness is the quality of being friendly, generous, and considerate. It can be a small act like sharing or it can be a big act, like buying a special gift. Just do something nice.

— DAY 19 —

Let your favorite song or beat transport you to your happy place.

Music is one of the most healing modalities of them all because there is the right type of music for everyone.

As each day comes to us refreshed and anew, so does my gratitude renew itself daily. The sun over the horizon is my grateful heart dawning upon a blessed world.
-Adabella Radici

Today I am grateful for...

DAY 19 : GRATITUDE ACTIVITY

Use Music to Lighten your Mood

As humans, we have the unique ability to change our experience or mood in an instant. Have you ever been in the middle of a conversation when suddenly your favorite song starts playing? Magically, you forget whatever you were saying and begin humming or singing the song. If you are really bold, you start snapping your fingers and moving your body. The edges of your mouth turn up and you are transported to happiness.

This is a perfect example of how a song can instantly change your attitude and bring about instant joy.

Music is something I use to raise my spirits whenever I'm down and have to snap out of it in a hurry. It is a true lift to my body and mind!

Today, I want you to find one of your favorite songs and play it. Let yourself listen to the beat and the words. Let it transport you to a happy place, a thankful place, a grateful place.

— DAY 20 —

Where would we be without the support of our communities?

When you share your favorite quote with people you know, it opens uplifting conversation.

Blessed are those that can give without remembering and receive without forgetting.
-*Author Unknown*

Today I am grateful for...

DAY 20 :GRATITUDE ACTIVITY

Take it to Social Media

We are almost three weeks into our 30 Daes of Gratitude program. Now, let's take our gratitude to social media. Let's flood the news feeds with great inspirational quotes.

Choose a quote that you love. It can be about anything. It doesn't have to be about gratitude. It just has to have a special meaning for you. Share it. Post it on Facebook, Twitter, LinkedIn, Instagram or YouTube. If you are not on social media, text it to a friend or a group of friends.

It is so lovely to share an inspirational quote with someone who might appreciate it. If you don't have a quote that you love, you can pick one from this program or look one up.

Another option is to call a friend and ask them to share their favorite quote. Sharing can be finding out someone else's favorite if you don't have one of your own.

— DAY 21 —

Show someone you are thinking about them.

Dopamine is another brain chemical that's released as part of a rewards program. When you feel like you're doing something good for another, it stimulates the reward system in the brain.

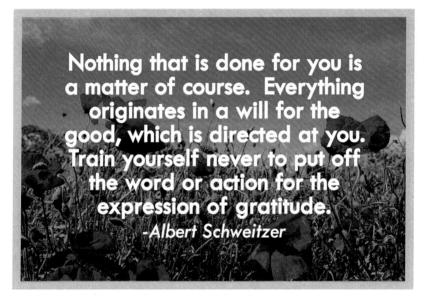

Nothing that is done for you is a matter of course. Everything originates in a will for the good, which is directed at you. Train yourself never to put off the word or action for the expression of gratitude.
-Albert Schweitzer

Today I am grateful for...

DAY 21 : GRATITUDE ACTIVITY

Write a Thank You Note

My Grammy was very big on etiquette! When I was a young girl, she taught me to hand write thank you notes. This practice of writing thank you notes is one of the things I have learned to cherish.

This practice is one I cherish because it allows me to say thank you for gifts and acts of kindness that touch me. I also cherish it because my friends who receive them appreciate the time and consideration that goes into writing a personal note. Personal, handwritten notes are so much more valuable than the normal junk mail most of us receive every day.

Today, I want you to write a note or card to someone. It can be a thank you note or just a 'thinking of you' note. You can use a plain sheet of white paper or get fancy and buy a card, whatever feels good to you!

Once you have written it, put it in an envelope and send it off in the mail. It will be a sweet surprise for the recipient in a few days!

Let me know how it feels to write this cool note!

— DAY 22 —

Remember to enjoy the moment and savor it.

When you are in the present moment, you are not rewriting the past nor are you worried about your future. It is a place of contentment with the now.

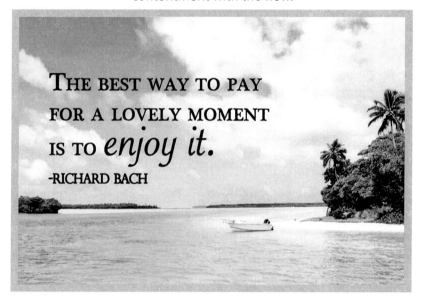

THE BEST WAY TO PAY FOR A LOVELY MOMENT IS TO *enjoy it.*
-RICHARD BACH

Today I am grateful for...

DAY 22 : GRATITUDE ACTIVITY

Stop and Smell the Roses

My Grammy loved gardening. She had many different types of roses in her front yard and tended to them until she was in her 90s. As she became less mobile, I would cut a few roses and bring them inside and put them on the dining room table where she could see them and enjoy their fragrance. She would look at them and smile, enjoying so much being able to be with them again.

For me, it brought a new meaning to the idea of taking time to stop and smell the roses.

If you like flowers and it's possible, I would like you to treat yourself to a floral bouquet. You can cut them off a bush or buy them from a store. Put them where you will see and enjoy them. Perhaps they will sit on your desk, on your dining room table, or even on your kitchen counter.

If you don't like flowers, pick something small that you do like and put it somewhere where you can see it. Ideas include a candle, a small figurine or a cute card with a quote on it.

Take moments during the day to stop and just enjoy the gift that you have given yourself. Enjoy the moment and savor it.

— DAY 23 —

Always remember to count your blessings.

Whatever we focus our attention on is what potentiates in our life.

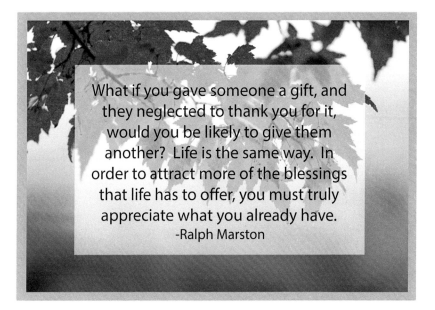

What if you gave someone a gift, and they neglected to thank you for it, would you be likely to give them another? Life is the same way. In order to attract more of the blessings that life has to offer, you must truly appreciate what you already have.
-Ralph Marston

Today I am grateful for...

DAY 23 : GRATITUDE ACTIVITY

Make a List of Gratitude

The movie 'The Secret' was the first time I learned about the law of attraction. The law of attraction states that our thoughts are the beginning point to creating things in our lives. So whatever our thoughts focus on, good or bad, will begin to show up in our lives. The more we focus on positive or grateful thoughts, the more positive or gratitude experiences we will have in our lives.

Today, I would like you to make a list of all the blessings that you have received in the last 24 hours. Please make sure your list has at least 10 items on it. I suggest that you take three minutes to review your day. Start by closing your eyes, take a few deep breaths and think back to the beginning of yesterday.

Briefly, think through your day to find all the blessings that occurred. Then give thanks for them. **Here is a sample from my day yesterday, all before 1pm:**

- I woke up next to my love and he kissed me on my forehead before heading out to exercise
- I called one of my best friends to see if I could join her for church – she said YES!
- We got to church early and sat in the main sanctuary (we are never early, always on overflow)
- We found a parking spot close by (which never happens probably because we are always late to church)!
- There was a guest minister, named one of the top 10 preachers in the country
- Some of our friends from an hour away were there.
- I bought some delicious fresh bread as a treat for the house
- I had lunch with my Godfather – who picked up the tab!
- I found the perfect thank you gifts for special friends
- I found a hat to keep me warm from the wind!

You get the picture! As you review your day, see the small things you usually miss that are blessings in disguise. It will lift your mood.

— DAY 24 —

Take a moment to make others feel seen and acknowledged.

Older people are a great reservoir of knowledge and they are often ignored or overlooked. Take a few minutes to spend time with an older person and find out about their life.

> *Gratitude can transform common days into thanksgivings, turn routine jobs into joy, and change ordinary opportunities into blessings.*
> -William Arthur Ward

Today I am grateful for...

DAY 24 : GRATITUDE ACTIVITY

Find Something Small to Share

I lived with my Grammy during the last four years of her life. It was an amazing experience to witness the gratitude she felt for the company, attention, affection, and just to be recognized as a human being at such an advanced age.

Many times, elderly people are not seen or acknowledged. Whenever my friends came to visit me, I always made sure that they spent a few minutes talking with Grammy. She loved it and they loved it too! She was so grateful for the company and the chance to tell stories and be acknowledged.

Today, I would like you to say something nice or do something nice for an older person. If you have young children, have them spend some time with grandparents. If they're far away, have them FaceTime or set up a zoom call. Find some small kindness to share with an older person. Let them know you're part of their life and you acknowledge their presence.

— DAY 25 —

When you are feeling deep gratitude, there is no space for negativity.

You can't feel negativity and positivity at the same time.
You have to choose one emotion at a time.

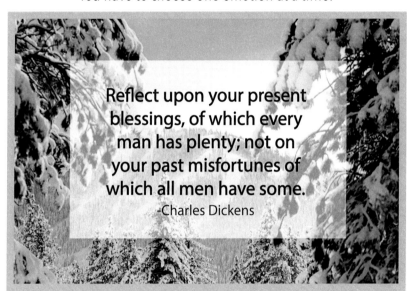

Reflect upon your present blessings, of which every man has plenty; not on your past misfortunes of which all men have some.
-Charles Dickens

Today I am grateful for...

DAY 25 : GRATITUDE ACTIVITY

Be Impeccable with your Words

Have you ever heard some juicy gossip that you wanted to share with everyone you know?

We have all had times where we hear a story about someone else and want to spread it by telling it again.

NOW have you ever been the person that everyone was talking about? It is not fun, and often cruel, when you are on the other side of the story. How did it make you feel? Vulnerable? Hurt? Shocked? Angry? None of these are good feelings to experience.

When you are feeling deep gratitude, you will not feel the need to talk negatively or gossip about someone else. Gratitude allows you to tell a happy and hopeful story about yourself or someone else.

Today, I want you to think about the stories you plan to share before you share them. Try to remember to be thoughtful with your words. Be impeccable with them.

In the book, *The Four Agreements*, Don Miguel Ruiz talks about being impeccable with your words. Today, watch your words. Be kind with your words and be thankful for them. Use your words to uplift others.

— DAY 26 —

We always have a choice to complain or to be grateful.

We have a richness in our thoughts. When we choose gratitude, we are rich and when we choose complaints we are poor. Do you want your thoughts each day to be rich or poor?

"Gratitude is riches. Complaint is poverty."
—Doris Day

Today I am grateful for...

DAY 26 : GRATITUDE ACTIVITY

A Complaint Free Day

Years ago, Will Bowen came to speak about his new program at our church. The program was called 'a complaint free world', which later became his book, *A Complaint Free World: How to Stop Complaining and Start Enjoying the Life You Always Wanted.*

In his program, he challenges us to not complain for 30 consecutive days. The first time I tried the program, it took me three months to get through 20 consecutive days without complaining. It was amazing how often I found things, both big and small, to complain about without realizing it.

Mr. Bowen initiated an easy activity. He brought rubber bracelets for us to wear and each time we caught ourselves complaining we were to move the bracelet from one wrist to the other. The goal was to keep the bracelet on one wrist for 30 days, signaling that you had not complained for 30 days.

Complaining is insidious. We probably don't realize how often we do it. Although we can have dozens of small complaints during the day, we only think about big complaints. For a little while, we'll think about complaints instead of gratitude, just to remind us that we always have a choice - to complain or be grateful.

Today, I would like you to take a loose rubber band or a hair tie or bracelet and put it on one wrist. Every time you notice that you are complaining move the "bracelet" from one wrist to the other. Notice how many times you move it during the day.

Complaining about the weather – oh it's so hot or cold - is a complaint. Griping about traffic or waiting in line – still complaints. See if you can notice at the end of the day how many complaints you made during the day. Can you have fewer the next day?

— DAY 27 —

*Feel gratitude for the opportunity
to try or learn about new things.*

It takes courage to try new things. When you have the courage to
try something new, you conquer fear.

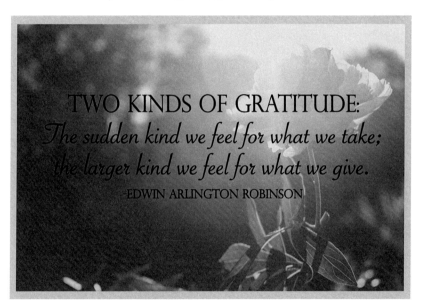

TWO KINDS OF GRATITUDE:
*The sudden kind we feel for what we take;
the larger kind we feel for what we give.*
-EDWIN ARLINGTON ROBINSON

Today I am grateful for...

DAY 27 : GRATITUDE ACTIVITY

Learn Something New

Have you ever listened to a friend tell you about something they have done and been inspired to try something new yourself?

This summer, a friend called me to tell me he was in town for the day and invited me to go tubing with him in an hour. I had no time to think about it and had to make a split-second decision. I said yes! Four hours later we were floating down the Potomac River having the best time of the summer! I had never gone tubing before and now I will definitely go back again.

I was so thankful to have tried something new!

Be willing to learn something new or try something new today.

It could be anything! You might decide to eat in a restaurant that you have passed by for months or try a new dish at your usual spot. Maybe you could enroll in a class you think might be interesting or read a book by an unfamiliar author. Maybe you will walk into a crafts store and buy paints and an easel!

Try something new and be grateful for the experience.

— **DAY 28** —

Gratitude helps solve problems

We have the most to give when we are giving to others from our
genuine desire to make their lives better.

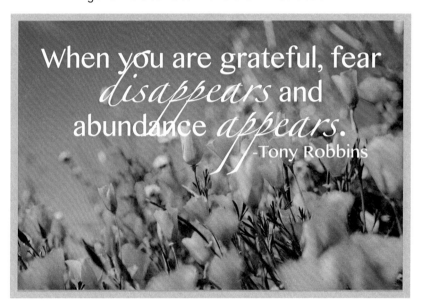

When you are grateful, fear *disappears* and abundance *appears.*
-Tony Robbins

Today I am grateful for...

DAY 28 : GRATITUDE ACTIVITY

Give a Little More

Several years ago, I was feeling really down. I wasn't making enough money to pay my bills and I was afraid I was going to lose my practice. I didn't know what to do. I started to feel fearful and overwhelmed.

Days went by and I couldn't shake my anxiety and depression. Instead of wallowing in self-pity, I decided to volunteer at my church to help feed families that didn't have enough food. After just one day at the church, I had such gratitude for what I had! My situation didn't change, but my perspective on it certainly did!

The experience helped me look at my situation with new eyes. I was able to figure out how to change my situation. Gratitude helped me and it can help you. Look for an organization that you can help accomplish its mission. It may help children, the homeless or veterans. If possible, sign up and volunteer to help the organization.

— DAY 29 —

earn to relax and become grateful for
e simple things right in front of you.

Breathing is the simplest, most powerful form of gratitude for life.

We often take for granted
the very things that most
deserve our gratitude.
-Cynthia Ozick

Today I am grateful for...

DAY 29 : GRATITUDE ACTIVITY

Take 10 Deep Breaths

About 18 years ago, I began practicing vigorous yoga in which I had to learn to breathe in a certain way or risk fainting. Then, about 12 years ago, I started meditating. Again, I had to learn to pay close attention to my breathing.

In each of these activities, I became aware of the power of each breath. My breath helped me calm my mind and body. Just by closing my eyes and focusing on filling my lungs with air, I learned to relax and become grateful for the simple things right in front of me.

Today, I want you to take one minute to take 10 deep breaths. Simply close your eyes and deeply inhale. Perhaps you count to four as you inhale and then breathe out to the count of four as you exhale.

Do this 10 times in a row. After your last breath, check in with your whole body to see how you feel. Do you notice that you feel calmer and more relaxed?

Have gratitude for how this simple exercise has helped you to feel better.

— DAY 30 —

Watch your gratitude change and evolve.

In mindfulness practices like gratitude, you change over time and don't even notice it. Spend a few minutes reviewing your last 30 days.

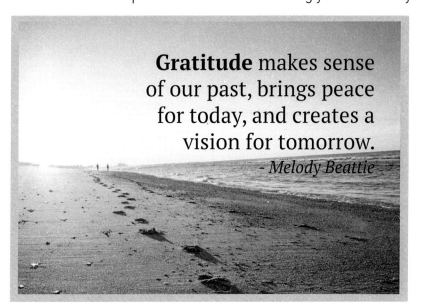

Gratitude makes sense of our past, brings peace for today, and creates a vision for tomorrow.
- *Melody Beattie*

Today I am grateful for...

DAY 30 : GRATITUDE ACTIVITY

Journaling Again

One of the things that inspired me to create this program was a study by The University of California, Berkeley in which researchers looked at over 1,000 people who wrote in gratitude journals. **Here are the benefits they observed:**

• Subjects had stronger immune systems
• They were less bothered by aches and pains
• They had lower blood pressure
• They exercised more and took better care of their health
• They slept longer and felt more refreshed upon waking
• They had higher levels of positive emotions
• They were more alert, alive, and awake
• They experienced more joy and pleasure
• They had more optimism and happiness
• They were more helpful, generous, and compassionate
• They were more forgiving
• They were more outgoing
• They felt less lonely and isolated

These are all wonderful benefits. I hope over the last 30 days, you're starting to see these things show up in your own life!

I want you to revisit Day 2's activity - to keep a gratitude journal. If you have decided to keep a journal, look back over the last 30 days to see how your gratitude has changed or evolved during this program. If you have not been keeping a journal, consider finding your journal from Day 2 and begin to write in it again. Even though the program is completed you may realize the success and impact it's had in your life and restart it at another time.

CONGRATULATIONS!

First, I want you to acknowledge that you have put yourself and your health first. Notice any benefits that you have gained have improved your self esteem and confidence. Notice how your relationships have improved with family or co-workers. Notice how your views and perspectives have changed for the better. Making yourself a priority, even for a few minutes a day, is a game changer for your life.

It has been such a joy to share this gratitude program with you! My hope is that you have been inspired to find more gratitude in your life. I hope your mood has been elevated and your health has improved. Gratitude changes perspectives on how you see the world. Even better, gratitude has been proven to support improved physical healing as well.

It is my hope that this 30 Dae by Dae guide has enhanced the quality of your life in many different ways.

If you have enjoyed this program, you are probably thinking… what's next?

Please look over the 30 Dae by Dae guide of activities and find one or two that you really enjoyed. Start implementing them on a regular basis to continue the flow of gratitude into your heart and mind. Consider this guide as a tool in your new naturopathic medicine kit. If you noticed a change in your health and attitude, then you are ready to learn more about how naturopathic medicine can continue to deepen your level of health.

If you have not done so already, go to our website, healthydaes.com, and sign up for our newsletter so you can learn about other programs and offerings we share throughout the year.

You will gain access to online programs, webinars, live events and private sessions to help you foster vibrant health in every aspect of your life! Become part of my community and learn more ways to infuse fun and healthy living into your daily routine!

Thank you so much for taking a few moments out of your day to participate in this healing guide.

To Your One Sweet Life,
Dr. Dae

DR. DAE'S BIOGRAPHY

Dr. Dae believes that the key to finding happiness and fulfillment is knowing it is okay to put yourself first and choose health as your number one priority. When you do, you are able to show up more powerfully in every aspect of your life – professionally, personally and in your community.

Dr. Dae works with individuals who are struggling with health issues such as weight gain, diabetes, thyroid problems and issues around menopause. These individuals often don't realize their health issues are stemming from hormonal imbalances that have not been addressed or properly treated.

Dr. Dae is an expert in using lifestyle as medicine to reduce chronic disease. Her *Replenish. Restore. Reclaim.* framework proves that diminished health and energy can be reversed with proactive choices, at any age.

Dr. Dae received her Naturopathic Medical degree from the University of Bridgeport's College of Naturopathic medicine in 2002. She completed her naturopathic boards in 2003 and has been practicing in Washington, D.C. for the last 18 years.

Dr. Dae is a licensed Naturopathic Doctor in Washington, D.C. and treats patients virtually all over the world.

Dr. Dae is committed to helping people learn how to create health in every area of their life. As a result, Dr. Dae has created books, electronic books and online courses to empower people to take back control of their health. To learn more about Dr. Dae's practice, products and online courses, visit her website at healthydaes.com.